Management Speak

S0-DZN-696

What managers say / What they mean

IS SURVIVOR
PUBLISHING

Management Speak

Published by IS Survivor Publishing, 6272 Sequoia Circle, Eden Prairie, Minnesota 55346, (952) 949-2444.

Visit our Web site at www.issurvivor.com.

Management Speak

First printing 2005

ISBN 978-0-9749354-1-6

LCCN 2005935650

Book design, cover design and production by Tim Bitney

Management Speak

Dedication

This book is dedicated to a lot of people. I can't name them, for two reasons. First, it would read like the Academy Awards Acceptance Speech from Hell, and second, half requested anonymity.

So we'll do it *en masse*. This book would literally not have been possible had it not been for the outpouring of contributions from a host of enthusiastic readers, whose discerning ears and perceptive minds allowed me to do nothing more than receive e-mails, and cut and paste into my database. Which wasn't as easy as it sounds.

Have you ever tried to cut and paste while laughing like a hyena?

Management Speak

Acknowledgements

Let's keep this short. You don't care anyway - you want to get to the ManagementSpeak section, and are only reading this out of guilt, right? So …

That this book exists at all is due to the efforts of Tim Bitney, my partner in publishing crime. Tim designed the cover, selected the ManagementSpeaks that grace the contents, laid everything out, and otherwise took care of the all the aggravating details that are the difference between good intentions and something you can put in gift wrap for your friends (a very good idea, by the way!).

Probably, it also wouldn't exist had it not been for William M. Gaines, the publisher of *Mad Magazine*, and Al

Acknowledgements

Jaffe, who wrote the Mad book that started it all so many years ago (I think - and if I'm remembering wrong, he wrote a bunch of other great stuff for *Mad*, so he still deserves mention.)

Thanks, Tim, for putting this together. Bill, Al ... I owe you big time for the inspiration, and for the part you played in my formative years.

Heck, had it not been for *Mad*, I'd have never known what an axolotl is.

Introduction

It began, as so much began, with *Mad Magazine*. More specifically, it began with a book: *What People Say and What They Really Mean* (or something like that - it was a long time ago). The book included such gems as:

What they say: "It isn't the money. It's the principle of the thing.

What they mean: "It's the money."

For a young lad trying to figure out the world, it was a field guide to adult behavior.

Then came grad school. In between bouts of research and grading papers, a friend handed me one of those photocopies of photocopies people used to get before the era of personal

Introduction

computers, e-mail, and the World Wide Web. It was the science version of my *Mad* book, containing helpful translations of common phrases found in published research:

Published phrase: "It is well known that …"

Translation: "I was too lazy to look up the original reference, but …"

The truth is out. I didn't invented the genre, or much of anything else, other than the word *ManagementSpeak*. That's mine, so far as I can tell. Maybe I should have trademarked it. If I had, though, I'd have had to call it *ManagementSpeak®*, which would have looked … the word "dopey" comes to mind.

It happened like this. In 1996 I started a weekly column in *InfoWorld*. It was called the *IS Survival Guide*. It wasn't about technology - unusual for an IT trade publication.

Introduction

Instead, it was about handling the organizations that manage technology. My goal was to write a column that would help CIOs succeed. I figured it should be original enough, and entertaining enough, to keep them awake long enough to finish my 775 words of wisdom.

What better to start off a column like this than a popular management phrase and its translation? Figuring I had everything to gain and nothing to lose, I gave it a shot, borrowing a key management concept from the world of leveraged buyouts. "They get rich using other people's money," I mused. "Why can't I get people to think I'm clever using other people's wit?"

So at the bottom of my first column, I said, "I'm collecting examples of ManagementSpeak (ManagementSpeak: "I'm not saying no, but I'm certainly not saying yes." Translation: "No."). I'll publish the winners (and their definitions) in future columns."

My editors hated the idea. "What if you don't get enough submissions?" they asked. "What if they want you to pay them?" "What if … what if … what if …"

Which recalled another key management concept, this time from the movie *Little Big Man:* Every enterprise involves a particle of risk [1].

The risk was short-lived. We ran the first column and it was like I'd turned on a fire hose. Examples poured in. Some

---

1 What - you thought most important business concepts come from business people or the business punditocracy? Not a chance. You can't trust those people - they use too much ManagementSpeak. Mostly, I find the best management ideas come from such sources as medieval generals, stand-up comics, *Hill Street Blues* and *Star Trek* (don't believe me? My friend Wess Roberts wrote a book titled *Make It So: Leadership Lessons from Star Trek the Next Generation*).

Introduction

submitters requesting anonymity, understandably fearing retribution. Others delighted at the idea of claiming a few moments of fame out of their promised fifteen minutes.

And I get credit for it! Yes, I do sometimes tweak, or even re-write the translation. Occasionally I even slip one of my own in. Mostly, my role in all of this is maintaining the database, making sure it's adequately backed up.

This would be the end of the story, and the introduction, were it not for a letter I received that turned into one of my favorite columns:

Dear Bob,

I know this is a rather odd question, but I need your help with Management Speak. No, it's not translating it, it's me translating to it!

I've been told that although I speak very well to

Introduction

and/or with end-users, I need to work more on talking
with upper management. Three different managers
have suggested this, so for the sake of my career and
IS survival, I'm taking them seriously.

I'm pretty sure the very thing my manager wants
is what you lampoon in your columns. Do you have
any suggestions on learning how to translate into
Management Speak instead of your normal practice of
translating from it? Just as important, can you tell me
how to not snicker while I'm doing it?

Dancing around issues and trying to put a
positive spin on everything, even when they are
potential issues that need to be addressed, seems
rather hypocritical. However, in the interest of my
career, I have to at least try to overcome this

Introduction

particular "weakness." Any suggestions, thoughts, or comments would be greatly appreciated.

- Talkin' Trash in Tennessee

Welcome to the wonderful world of ManagementSpeak. Whether you simply peruse the 130 gems that follow to enjoy the chuckles, as a field guide to what They're really trying to tell you, to give you some guidance on how to pass as one of Them, or, to discover the awful truth - that you've become one of Them ... whatever your motives, you have the same two assignments:

Assignment #1: Visit www.issurvivor.com and subscribe to the successor to the original IS Survival Guide, if you haven't already. It's called *Keep the Joint Running*. It's

Introduction

free and I don't sell my lists, so you have nothing to lose.

Assignment #2: Send me some examples of your own! You know what they say, after all - you can never be too rich, too good looking, or have too many examples of ManagementSpeak on hand. Send them to **managementspeak@issurvivor.com**.

Besides, if I'm going to publish another of these next year you might enjoy a chance at your own few moments of fame.

- Bob Lewis

66 Milestone celebrations are passé. 99

Translation

Morale-schmorale. If you want a pizza, buy it yourself.

— This contributor decided to remain anonymous, and to buy herself a pizza.

Management Speak

" This merger will result in synergy between our companies which fully utilizes our combined infrastructure and strategic planning. "

Translation

All of you are out of jobs, but I don't care because I have a golden parachute.

— This contributor, lacking his own golden parachute, remains anonymous.

Management Speak

> 66 I've asked Bill to take the lead on this project. 99

Translation

You need to take me golfing more often, George.

— This anonymous contributor got published because he took me golfing. (No, not really.)

Management Speak

66 I didn't understand the e-mail you said you sent. Can you give me a quick summary? 99

Translation

I still can't figure out how to start the e-mail program.

— Thanks to reader Jason Gill.

Management Speak

66 It's a no brainer. 99

Translation

It's a perfect decision for me to handle.

— Thanks to the anonymous reader who provided this entry.

Management Speak

66 I'm glad you asked me that. 99

Translation

Public Relations has written a carefully phrased answer.

— Thanks to reader Ben Cohen, who provided this, paraphrased from a Chicago Bar Association speaker.

Management Speak

66 We have an opportunity. 99

Translation

You have a problem.

— Thanks to reader Brian Redine.

Management Speak

66 The system has to be flexible. 99

Translation

We don't know what the hell we want.

— The contributor of this ManagementSpeak has requested
  anonymity. We can all understand why.

Management Speak

66 Human Resources 99

Translation

A bulk commodity, like lentils or cinder blocks.

— Thanks to Andrew Donovan-Shead.

Management Speak

66 I don't disagree. 99

Translation

I disagree.

— Thanks to George Behr for the quotation and translation.

18

Management Speak

66 You obviously put a lot of work into this. 99

Translation

This is awful.

Management Speak

66 Individual Contributor 99

Translation

Employee who does real work.

— Thanks to reader Juergen Rudnick for this winner.

Management Speak

66 Cost of ownership has become a significant issue in desktop computing. 99

Translation

We want all of the benefits and none of the costs.

— Our contributor this wants to remain anonymous.

Management Speak

66 We have to leverage our resources. 99

Translation

You're working weekends.

— Thanks to reader Andy Coyle for this addition to our
language instruction program.

22

Management Speak

66 I'll never lie to you. 99

Translation

The truth will change frequently.

— This donor wisely prefers to remain anonymous.

Management Speak

66 It's not possible. It's impractical.
It won't work. 99

Translation

I don't know how to do it.

— Reader Tom Warburton provided this contribution.

Management Speak

❝ You will be fully empowered to make decisions on this project. **❞**

Translation

You'll get no support from me.

— From an anonymous reader who apparently doesn't feel quite empowered enough.

Management Speak

66 Our leadership team determined that we need to establish metrics for our key processes to verify that we continuously improve. 99

Translation

Let's produce a blizzard of numbers large enough to make the leadership's eyes glaze over, while not actually measuring anything useful or informative.

— An anonymous reader provided this vocabulary builder.

Management Speak

66 I feel strongly both ways. 99

Translation

*I don't want to delegate the decision to you,
but I'm certainly not competent to make it
myself.*

— Reader Mark Hoffman provided this phrase and its
interpretation.

Management Speak

66 Our business is going through a
paradigm shift. 99

Translation

*We've no idea what we have been doing, but
in the future we shall do something
completely different.*

— Tim Stevens provided this interpretation.

Management Speak

"It's just a proof of concept."

Translation

This is something I wanted to work on, but knew you'd say no if I asked.

— This contributor didn't explain whether he was speaker or listener, but did want his identity concealed.

Management Speak

66 We see no changes in management at this time. 99

Translation

We're planning a bloodbath.

— Thanks to reader David Greusel for this addition to our phrase book.

Management Speak

66 That only happens once
in a blue moon. 99

Translation

*We'll worry about it when one of our big
name accounts brings it up.*

— Thomas Campbell put this unit of time into perspective.

Management Speak

66 We want you to be happy. 99

Translation

You'll do it our way and you'll like it.

— Thanks to Mike Miller for pointing this out

Management Speak

66 The project team has been working diligently on the release and has made significant progress. 99

Translation

The project is behind schedule.

— Alan Chattaway apparently watched this project from a safe distance.

Management Speak

66 I know we've empowered you,
but that doesn't mean you can say
no. 99

Translation

Too bad.

— David Knoblich, offers a useful phrase for those special
situations.

Management Speak

66 This was the most successful project I've ever participated in! 99

Translation

Everyone liked the report. Even better, the company changed direction before we had to make it work.

— This contributor's survival appears to hinge on his/ her continued anonymity.

Management Speak

66 We have made some changes to our benefits package I think you will be very excited about. 99

Translation

Boy, are you in for a surprise when you try to file a claim.

— This contributor figures anonymity will enhance his chance for survival.

Management Speak

66 We don't have time for solutions.
I need an answer! 99

Translation

Tell me what I want to hear, immediately!

— Greg Linde explains the difference between solutions and
answers.

Management Speak

66 We're doing the same thing, but in a different way. 99

Translation

We've completely changed our minds.

— This contributor wouldn't change his mind - he insists on remaining anonymous.

Management Speak

66 You have the unique ability to describe technology in an easy to understand format. 99

Translation

We had no idea you were such a simpleton when we hired you.

— Do you think Riley T. Bell is sending me a message?

Management Speak

66 That's an intriguing notion that merits additional thought on the part of our best people. 99

Translation

No.

— Roger Simpson explains the value of "additional thought".

Management Speak

66 That's an innovative solution. 99

Translation

We've never done it that way before, so if it fails, I never heard of you OR the project.

— John Pfeifer delivers an innovative alternative to the standard "Mission Impossible" disclaimer.

Management Speak

❝ Your project isn't dead, we're just putting it in our toolbox of components that we can use in the future. **❞**

Translation

It's dead.

— Michael P. Kearney 'componentizes' mortality, thereby turning it into an ActiveX control.

Management Speak

" Do it the right way. "

Translation

Do it my way, no matter how stupid.

— This contributor, finding nobility in having common cause with
his peers, asks to be known only as "Every Programmer."

Management Speak

66 I've been thinking about the situation and it troubles me. 99

Translation

I'm sorry you found out what we've been doing behind your back.

— David Paul explains the true nature of regret.

Management Speak

66 I like the way you think. 99

Translation

I'm going to take credit for your ideas.

— With luck I'll get credit for Toby Velte's wit

45

Management Speak

66 We're going to place this project on hold for re-evaluation. 99

Translation

We've screwed up and we don't know how to fix it.

— Chris Klein places our faith in management's ability to communicate on hold.

46

Management Speak

66 It's an industry standard. 99

Translation

We have no clue why we do it this way.

— Todd Bailey explains the purpose of standards.

Management Speak

66 Let's keep our eye on the big picture. We can work out the technical details later. This is an opportunity we can't afford to miss. 99

Translation

I vaguely recall reading something about this in a magazine. I'm not sure what it means, or even if it is possible.

— We get a glimpse of the big picture from Jason Gill.

Management Speak

66 Our value proposition presents a unique opportunity for our customers and employees. 99

Translation

Opportunity for employees: Work more hours. Opportunity for customers: Spend more.

— Thanks to Bryan Mullinax for explaining the nature of opportunity.

Management Speak

66 We have to do it the way we've always done it, even if it is wrong, because changing it would cause too many problems. 99

Translation

Everybody involved in creating this monster is either dead, retired, or laid off.

— Revealing the name of this source would cause too many problems.

Management Speak

66 I'm trying to make the best use
of your time. 99

Translation

Get back to work!

— Matt Olson provided us with an fine example of the art — an
excellent use of his time.

Management Speak

❝ Our best course of action is
to defer this decision
for a few years. ❞

Translation

I'm going to retire before then.

— Dale McKinnon explains strategic decision-making.

Management Speak

66 Submit a Project Request Form and we will prioritize it with our other projects. 99

Translation

No.

— This anonymous contributor draws a verbal process map.

"You've done a great job. "

Translation

*I don't have a clue how you performed but
I've heard no bad reports.*

— Leonard R. Miller's contribution is a great job, don't you
think?

Management Speak

66 Successfully resolving
this problem is vital
to the company. 99

Translation

*Successfully resolving this problem is vital
to your continued employment
with this company.*

— Dana Persells shows how individual and corporate goals
align.

Management Speak

66 The best way to get a vision is to see what someone else is doing. **99**

Translation

Try to not get caught plagiarizing.

— Dan Rosen accounts for originality among business strategists.

Management Speak

66 In the real world ... 99

Translation

This happened to my wife's cousin's friend ...

— This contributor provides a healthy dose of reality.

Management Speak

66 Don't waste time worrying about layoffs. Just get back to work. 99

Translation

The sooner you get your work done, the sooner we can lay you off.

— Brian Crook explains the results of getting back to work.

Management Speak

66 I don't disagree with what you're saying. 99

Translation

I stopped listening to you five minutes ago.

— I don't disagree with Luther Walke's interpretation.

Management Speak

66 Tell me how we can improve our department so we can be more productive. 99

Translation

We want to find out who the troublemakers are.

— This contributor didn't want the troublemaker revealed ... he asked to remain anonymous.

Management Speak

66 Don't just bring me problems,
bring me solutions. 99

Translation

*I'm the cause of the problems, after all ...
why would you expect me to solve them?*

— This anonymous contributor solved one of my problems ...
he provided a very helpful translation.

Management Speak

66We're managing for change. 99

Translation

We have no idea where we're going
or what we're doing.

— Michael J. Austin demonstrates his sense of direction.

Management Speak

66 We need to leverage our
brand name. 99

Translation

*We're going to cut the quality,
raise the price and buy a TV ad.*

— In order to preserve his personal brand, this phrase-donor
has asked to remain anonymous.

Management Speak

66 We value your opinion. 99

Translation

Anything you say can and will be
used against you.

— While we value this opinion, we can't hold it against the
    contributor, as he chose to remain anonymous.

Management Speak

66 This is not a demotion. 99

Translation

This is a demotion.

— Because this week's contributor asked to remain
   anonymous, we'll never know whether it was one or not.

Management Speak

66 This new job title may be unusual, but it more accurately reflects your duties. 99

Translation

I don't want you to be able to find your job in a salary survey.

— This contributor is a "Product Analyst" from the Great Southwest ... does anyone know what that position pays?

Management Speak

66 Preliminary tests were
inconclusive. 99

Translation

*We couldn't even figure out how
to start it up.*

— Speaking of inconclusive, this contributor never gave
permission to mention his name.

Management Speak

66 We have set an
aggressive schedule, but we
have faith in you. 99

Translation

*This is an impossible schedule and we are
already behind. Risk of failure is high, but
we plan on making you responsible.*

— This contributor felt responsible enough without being
identified here.

Management Speak

66 We have an evolving
business model. 99

Translation

*We're in the red and don't
know how to fix it.*

— Stirling Rasmussen demonstrates his expertise in strategic
business analysis.

Management Speak

66 I would like to say that it's true.
I'm not going to say that
it's not true. 99

Translation

I don't know.

— J. W. Jensen recognizes the truth.

Management Speak

66 Cost-synergy objectives. 99

Translation

Employee layoffs.

— This entry came from a reader who doesn't want to
contribute to any cost-synergy objectives

Management Speak

66 Think outside the box. 99

Translation

There's no money in the box.

— This contributor figured that by remaining anonymous, he could avoid the box altogether.

Management Speak

66 Since you're our expert
in this field, we would like you
to mentor Joe in it. 99

Translation

*We would like you to train Joe
to be your replacement.*

— This anonymous contributor, on the other hand, is
irreplaceable.

Management Speak

66 Honesty is the best policy. 99

Translation

Well, lying didn't work ...

— Dale McKinnon tells us the honest truth (which is, of course, the preferred kind).

Management Speak

66 There will be no cuts in personnel after the merger is completed. 99

Translation

Please don't leave until we decide who we want to lay off.

— I think we can guess why this contributor chose to remain anonymous.

Management Speak

66 We believe their career opportunities will be enhanced by the new strategic partnership. 99

Translation

They're outta here!

— This week's contributor chooses to remain anonymous to avoid enhanced career opportunities.

Management Speak

66 We are reassessing our strategy for this product while we focus on our core markets. 99

Translation

We're dropping it like a hot potato.

— This anonymous hero is reassessing the meaning of this bit of obfuscation.

Management Speak

66 I'd like your opinion. 99

Translation

*We've made a decision
and want to feel good about it.*

— An anonymous reader feels pretty good about sharing his
translation of this bit of management misdirection.

Management Speak

66 It's a training issue. 99

Translation

*We know the software is defective,
but it's easier to blame the users
than to fix it.*

— If you think this translation is defective, feel free to blame
the anonymous reader who contributed this entry.

Management Speak

66 The ideal employee should be a team player. 99

Translation

The ideal employee won't question the supervisor.

— The ideal employee won't question the supervisor.

66 It's a high level model. 99

Translation

It's wrong.

— This anonymous contributor is right.

Management Speak

66 Our customers are part of the team. 99

Translation

They're the test department.

— This anonymous contributor is part of the
ManagementSpeak Translation Team.

Management Speak

66 Don't thank us. It's the least
we could do. 99

Translation

*We tried to do less, but couldn't
get away with it.*

— Thanks to this contributor, who, by remaining anonymous,
did get away with it.

Management Speak

66 Work smarter. 99

Translation

Work harder.

— This anonymous contributor worked hard and smart on your behalf to figure out this translation.

Management Speak

66 I don't think you'd like that job. **99**

Translation

I don't want to hire you.

— Jeff Peterson does, however, get the job as translator.

Management Speak

> 66 Boy, we dodged a bullet on that one. 99

Translation

What's bad isn't that we shot ourselves in the foot. It's how fast we reloaded and fired again.

— Mike Laughon explains the source of enemy fire.

66 It pays to be flexible
in determining your needs. 99

Translation

Want what we give you.

— As it happens, we do want what Jack Ranby gave us — an excellent translation.

Management Speak

> " In this uncertain business climate we find it necessary to take actions that will enable us to maintain our position in the industry. "

Translation

We're certain that by laying off another 10% of our employees this quarter we'll avoid another 20% drop in our stock price.

— Ken Ries explains how to be certain in uncertain times.

Management Speak

66 I am confident our company
will be exonerated
of all charges. 99

Translation

*We can afford better lawyers and
more of them.*

— This contributor prefers anonymity to exoneration.

Management Speak

66 We are reworking our employee survey instrument to give more useful results. 99

Translation

We're going to keep rewriting the questions until we get the answers we want.

— John Pfeifer got his translation right on the first try.

90

Management Speak

" Check your titles at the door. "

Translation

We want to find out who the troublemakers are.

— Tom Raschke is a non-trouble-making contributor.

66 You don't want to know. 99

Translation

I don't want to tell you.

— David Beamer, on the other hand, did want you to know.

Management Speak

66 We don't have an organization chart. We're a start-up. 99

Translation

We have no idea who's supposed to do what, when, or to whom.

— This contributor understood what he was supposed to do: Report what he heard to the rest of us.

Management Speak

66 Despite an unfavorable economic climate, we decided to go ahead with the Holiday Party in order to boost employee morale. 99

Translation

We couldn't get our deposit back.

— This contributor remains anonymous due to his company's unfavorable linguistic climate.

Management Speak

66 That would have to be a team decision. 99

Translation

I've already told you how I want it done.
Why are you still standing there?

— Our contributor's desire to remain anonymous was,
   however, an individual decision

Management Speak

66 We need to establish uniform practices across the enterprise. 99

Translation

*We see what you're doing,
and we want you to stop it.*

— John Pfeifer would like to stop the uniform practice of obfuscatory exposition.

Management Speak

66 We are not having any layoffs. 99

Translation

The layoffs won't be announced until next week.

— Bill Adams announces the proper translation.

Management Speak

66 Are there other options? 99

Translation

I don't understand the option you just explained.

— Buddy Ackerman understood what was said perfectly.

Management Speak

66 Quality is free. 99

Translation

*We have no intention of investing
in our business.*

— This contributor invested a high-quality ManagementSpeak
translation ... for free.

Management Speak

66 It's the right thing to do. 99

Translation

Do this or we'll get our butts sued.

— Dennis Hurlbut did the right thing by providing this
translation.

100

Management Speak

66 We're launching a quick
win effort. 99

Translation

*If I don't deliver results soon,
I'm fired.*

— This contributor delivered a solid result ... for us, at least.

Management Speak

❝ Ours is a dynamic business and they need to understand it. **❞**

Translation

We don't care if anything gets finished.
We just care that everything is urgent.

— Thanks to this anonymous contributor for a dynamic translation.

Management Speak

66 Don't spend more than ten
minutes on it. 99

Translation

Do it in your own time.

— Mike Baxter translated this for us in his own time.

Management Speak

" We really need to break down the silos in our organization. "

Translation

I want someone else to do the work our department is responsible for.

— Chip Gorman explains the semantics of silos.

Management Speak

66 We're homelanding this function. 99

Translation

We're bringing this business function back from India. We just realized that having this part of our infrastructure 12,500 miles away is risky.

— Steve Sacco homelanded this translation for us.

Management Speak

66 It's a legacy problem. 99

Translation

We have no idea how the thing works so we're blaming it on the people who built it because they aren't around to defend it.

— This anonymous contributor knows exactly how blamestorming works.

106

Management Speak

66 Trust me. 99

Translation

You're doomed.

— William Adams, PE, PhD, provided this erudite translation.

Management Speak

66 It is what it is. 99

Translation

I accept that I have no control in this behemoth of disorganized chaos. Why don't you?

— This translation, from an unnamed source, is quite a bit more than it is, don't you think?

108

66 We've got to control
expectations. 99

Translation

*We really screwed up, and took on more than
we can do. Now we've got to convince our
client not to can us.*

— Peter Bushman adjusts our expectations.

Management Speak

66 He plays a key role in
our process. 99

Translation

*He's the only one who knows anything
about this process.*

— This source, Mr. Jan McCollum isn't the only one who knows
the hidden meaning in this phrase.

Management Speak

66 Let's talk. 99

Translation

Be quiet and listen.

— This contributor was so quiet I never got his name.

Management Speak

66 People just don't like change. 99

Translation
My solution is worse than the problem.

— Richard Randles explains why people don't like change

66 You're being cynical. 99

You're right, but we don't want to admit it.

— This contributor might be cynical, but he's certainly right.

Management Speak

> ❝ I have some good news for you. ❞

Translation

I have some bad news for you, but with more spin on it than a Nolan Ryan curveball.

— Dale McKinnon spins in reverse.

Management Speak

66 Doing it the way you suggest would negatively impact the process we are trying to implement. 99

Translation

No, and no I won't give you a reason.

— Translating this entry as our contributor suggests will positively impact your understanding.

Management Speak

66 This isn't a cost-effective
solution. 99

Translation

*This is going to be charged to my
cost center.*

— Bill McIntosh supplies us with a very effective translation.

Management Speak

" Pick the low-hanging fruit. "

Translation

Do it the quick and stupid way — I'll be gone before the problems show up.

— This anonymous contributor picked some low-hanging fruit
   of his own — an easily translated phrase.

Management Speak

66 You're right on target. 99

Translation

You agree with me.

— This unnamed contributor explains the nature of accuracy.

118

Management Speak

66 One of our core values is to act
with a sense of urgency. 99

Translation

*This organization pays no attention to
anything until it's a crisis.*

— Pay attention to Craig McAllister.

Management Speak

66 I didn't realize I owned that issue. 99

Translation

I plan to sit on my butt.

— This anonymous contributor explains the relationship between ownership and sessility.

Management Speak

" We want to be flexible, but we're not going to compromise. "

Translation

Forget it.

— This, uttered by a former head of Eastern Airlines Machinists Union, is one of my dad's personal favorites.

Management Speak

66 It's in development. 99

Translation

We never thought of that ...
but we should have.

— Rob Chenault developed this translation for us.

122

Management Speak

66 We're evaluating the software. 99

Translation

The check is in the mail.
We're working hard on it.
Don't call us, we'll call you.

— Kim Boriskin evaluates this choice phrase for us.

Management Speak

66 We have a personality conflict. 99

Translation

You have a personality and I'm the only person in this organization who's allowed to.

— This contributor is keeping his identity, rather than his personality, under wraps.

Management Speak

" People are our greatest asset. "

Translation

People are our biggest expense item.

— The anonymous contributor who provided this week's
   linguistic asset wants to keep on being an expense item.

Management Speak

" Quality is an overhead expense and must be reduced. "

Translation

Management is an unnecessary expense but we'll keep funding it.

— Steve Jackson provided both the phrase and translation ... not that any translation was needed, of course.

126

Management Speak

66 Lean and Mean. 99

Translation

Famished and Feeble.

— Janet Jonas wins the prize for her translation of this overused and abused management cliche.

Management Speak

66 We have to face reality. 99

Translation

*We have to try a simplistic solution
to the mess our simplistic thinking
got us into.*

— This anonymous contributor provides a realistic translation.

Management Speak

66 We rely on our front-line personnel to discover innovative ways of getting the work done. 99

Translation

Two words: Budget Freeze.

— John Pfeifer is one of the front-line personnel.

Management Speak

66 We blundered into a solution. 99

Translation

Somebody else thought of the solution.

— This contributor, known only as "From Nashville," didn't have to blunder into this translation.

130

Management Speak

66 Our new reorganization will allow us to more effectively respond to the challenges we face in the current business environment. 99

Translation

Things are going to get worse before they get better.

— Chris Keating describes the biggest challenge of most business environments.

Management Speak

66 Our Vision ... 99

Translation

What I want.

— Richard Low's vision is for business leaders to be less grandiose.

Management Speak

66 This merger will provide a number of synergies to reap financial benefits to our bottom line. 99

Translation

I'm selling off my company stock now.

— This contributor provided no synergies — only the excellent financial benefits that accompany good investment advice.

Management Speak

66 We built this company on
innovation. 99

Translation

R&D is no longer necessary.

— As this anonymous contributor points out, innovative
interpretation continues to be necessary.

Management Speak

66 We're looking for a self-starter. 99

Translation

We want someone who shows up on time.

— John Priebe was enough of a self-starter to provide this example.

Management Speak

66 I'm just trying to be fair to everyone. 99

Translation

I'm rewriting the rules so I always win.

— This anonymous contributor gives us a fair translation.

136

Management Speak

66 I would really like this discussion
to come to an end. 99

Translation

*I know I'm wrong, but there's no way
I'm going to admit it.*

— Jim Ehrlich recognized the best way to end this discussion
— by reporting it to us, and what it meant.